A Note to Parents and Teachers

DK READERS is a compelling programme for beginning readers, designed in conjunction with literacy experts, including Maureen Fernandes, B.Ed (Hons). Maureen has spent many years teaching literacy, both in the classroom and as a specialist in schools.

Beautiful illustrations and superb full-colour photographs combine with engaging, easy-to-read text to offer a fresh approach to each subject in the series.

Each DK READER is guaranteed to capture a child's interest while developing his or her reading skills, general knowledge and love of reading.

The five levels of DK READERS are aimed at different reading abilities, enabling you to choose the books that are exactly right for your child:

Pre-level 1: Learning to read

Level 1: Beginning to read

Level 2: Beginning to read alone

D0268220

Level 3: Reading alone

Level 4: Proficient readers

The 'normal' age at which a child begins to read can be anywhere from three to eight years old, so these levels are only a general guideline.

No matter which level you select, you can be sure that you are helping your child learn to read, then read to learn!

Penguin Random House

Senior Editor Catherine Saunders
Designer Jon Hall
Senior Slipcase Designer Mark Penfound
Senior DTP Designer Kavita Varma
Senior Producer Alex Bell
Brand Manager Robert Perry
Managing Editor Sadie Smith
Design Manager Ron Stobbart
Creative Manager Sarah Harland
Art Director Lisa Lanzarini
Publisher Julie Ferris
Publishing Director Simon Beecroft

Reading Specialist
Maureen Fernandes

This edition published in 2015
First published in Great Britain in 2008
by Dorling Kindersley Limited,
80 Strand, London WC2R 0RL
A Penguin Random House Company

Slipcase UI: 001-286401-Apr/15

A CIP catalogue record for this book is available
from the British Library.

ISBN 978-1-4053-2855-5

Printed in China.

www.dk.com

A WORLD OF IDEAS:
SEE ALL THERE IS TO KNOW

Contents

DK READERS

PROFICIENT READERS 4

MARVEL
GREATEST BATTLES

Written by Matthew K Manning

The Heroes
Whether they earned their powers from a lab accident, intensive training, or just by a fluke of nature, the one quality that all Super Heroes share is the need to stand up for what is right.

Heroes and Villains

When evil men, women and creatures threaten innocent people or even the entire galaxy, it takes a Super Hero to stop them. Super Heroes come in all shapes and sizes and have amazing powers. Some can lift buildings, others can climb them. Some can see in the dark and others can fly though the air.

These amazing Super Heroes risk their lives to defeat wicked Super Villains. However, even a Super Hero's powers have limits. When the odds are stacked against them, one hero might not be enough. So Super Heroes must swallow their pride and join forces to fight for justice. Read on to learn about some fantastic heroes and their greatest battles.

Top Teams
Super Heroes often work best when they get together. The Avengers, X-Men and Fantastic Four are three famous Super Hero teams.

Super Powers
Spider-Man has
super strength
and agility. He
can also crawl
on walls and
ceilings, thanks
to his ability to
stick to most
surfaces.

Spider-Man

When shy high school student
Peter Parker was bitten by a
radioactive spider, he gained some
amazing new abilities. Peter wanted
to use these powers to help people so
he created a secret Super Hero
identity – Spider-Man.

Although Spider-Man usually fights alone, sometimes he needs help to battle villains. Over the years, Spider-Man has teamed up with a selection of fantastic Super Heroes whose powers rival his own. From battling Dr Doom with the Human Torch, to taking on the Red Skull alongside the awe-inspiring Captain America, Spidey has discovered that even Super Heroes need friends.

Ice Hot Friends
Spider-Man, Firestar and Iceman often find themselves allies, despite their very different personalities!

Daredevil
Spidey and Daredevil have joined forces on many occasions. They have even confided their secret identities to each other.

Maximum Carnage

Spider-Man faced one of his greatest challenges when Carnage escaped from his cell at the Ravencroft Institution. Carnage is the crazed alter ego of criminal Cletus Kasady. Carnage assembled a team of bizarre villains, ranging from the motherly Shriek to the terrifying Demogoblin and the ferocious Spider Doppelganger. These dangerous villains wreaked havoc on Manhattan until Spider-Man created a Super Hero team of his own to deal with them.

Carnage
His powers come from an alien symbiote and he thinks that people should do whatever they want, even murder.

Demogoblin
The mysterious Demogoblin rides on a glider which is capable of shooting fiery blasts at his opponents.

Demo's arsenal also includes pumpkin bombs.

With the help of heroes including Captain America, Firestar and the runaways-turned-Super Heroes Cloak and Dagger, Spider-Man managed to turn the tables on Carnage and his evil allies. But it wasn't until Spider-Man enlisted the aid of his old enemy Venom that he was able to truly defeat his foe. With Venom's help, Spidey was finally able to return Carnage to his maximum security cell.

Team Up
Although Venom helped Spider-Man to defeat Carnage, he escaped on the back of a truck soon after the battle was over. Venom did not want to go to jail for his past crimes.

The Incredible Hulk

When Dr Bruce Banner accidentally wandered onto a military testing ground for gamma radiation, he was caught in a massive explosion. The radiation transformed Bruce Banner into the Incredible Hulk. The Hulk is a creature of nearly limitless strength, but with a very limited temper! Although he tries to keep his anger under control, the Hulk has still come into conflict with many of his fellow heroes along the way.

The X-Factor
Hulk fought Cyclops, Iceman and Marvel Girl, before realising that they were on the same side!

Hulk vs Spidey
Spidey and the Hulk have fought many times. One time, Spider-Man had temporary cosmic abilities, which made him as strong as Hulk.

When Iron Man mistook the Hulk for a monster, he tried to subdue the giant brute. Hulk relied on his super strength to defeat Iron Man, but that would not be the last time these two heroes met. In fact, they would later form an uneasy alliance in the Avengers Super Team.

The angrier Hulk gets, the stronger he becomes!

The Abomination
When KGB agent Emil Blonsky exposed himself to gamma radiation, he became the Abomination. He has become one of Hulk's most persistent enemies.

The Fantastic Four

In some ways, the Fantastic Four are more like a family than a Super Hero team. The team are scientist Reed Richards and his wife Sue Storm, Sue's brother Johnny Storm and Reed's best friend, Ben Grimm.

Each member of the Fantastic Four has a special power.

Origins
The Fantastic Four acquired their powers when they were exposed to cosmic rays during an experimental space mission.

Back Up
Other heroes have joined the Fantastic Four when the core members were absent from duty, including: She-Hulk, Ms Marvel and Luke Cage.

Reed Richards' body is able to stretch as far as his imaginative mind. Perhaps the world's smartest man, Reed calls himself Mr Fantastic. His more reserved wife can become invisible at will and project force fields, so she goes by the name Invisible Woman. Johnny Storm can literally set his entire body on fire so he is dubbed the Human Torch. Finally, Ben Grimm, the dependable rock of the group, calls himself the Thing, due to his massive stone-like appearance and super strength.

Love Rivals
Namor, King of Atlantis, has deep feelings for the Invisible Woman. This has created a rivalry between him and her husband, Mr Fantastic!

Friendly Foes
Although the Human Torch and the Thing don't always get along, they can rely on each other in a real fight.

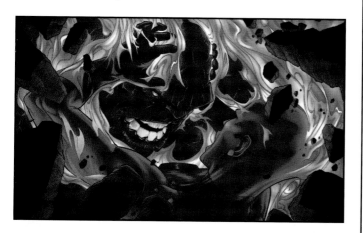

Dr Doom
Having suffered defeat at the FF's hands time and time again, Dr Doom used his scientific knowledge to try and ruin Reed and Sue's special day.

Fantastic Wedding

Reed Richards and Sue Storm very nearly didn't make it down the aisle. When Super Villain Dr Doom read of their forthcoming marriage, he saw the perfect opportunity for revenge on the Fantastic Four.

Mr Fantastic and the Invisible Woman had invited nearly every Super Hero in existence to come and celebrate with them. The evil Dr Doom rigged a machine to broadcast an 'inner voice' into the minds of dozens of villains. Under Doom's influence, fearsome rogues such as the Mole Man and the Mandarin began to attack the wedding guests. Thankfully a mysterious entity named the Watcher stepped in saved the day. He showed Mr. Fantastic how to send all the villains back in time with a sub-atronic time displacer.

Mole Man
The Mole Man and his army of Subterraneans were fought off by the original X-Men.

Guest List
The famous Super Heroes in attendance included Iron Man, Nick Fury, Captain America and Daredevil.

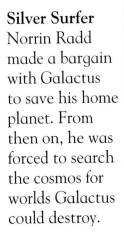

Galactus

Silver Surfer
Norrin Radd made a bargain with Galactus to save his home planet. From then on, he was forced to search the cosmos for worlds Galactus could destroy.

Amidst fires over the Manhattan skyline, the mysterious Silver Surfer suddenly appeared. The Surfer had come to make way for his master Galactus, a cosmic entity who devoured worlds. Galactus had Earth in his sights, and only the Fantastic Four stood in his way!

As the Four battled Galactus, the Watcher appeared once more and introduced Reed to the Ultimate Nullifier – the only weapon powerful enough to destroy Galactus. Later, the Silver Surfer joined the Fantastic Four and battled his former master. Galactus finally retreated back to the cosmos, but only after punishing the Surfer.

Fantastic Four
Galactus set up a life-energy draining device on top of the Fantastic Four's home, a skyscraper known as the Baxter Building.

Hunger

Galactus considers himself above mortal concerns and only cares about satisfying his hunger.

Heralds

Galactus has had many heralds over the years. Even the Fantastic Four's own Human Torch served him once.

More than just a Super Villain, Galactus is a universal force, like death or gravity.

Hulk vs Thing

When these two
Super Heroes meet, the
Earth moves. Literally!
Virtually equal in size
and strength, the Hulk and
the Thing have had some of
the longest and most
memorable fights in Super
Hero history.

Once a bizarre experiment
switched their minds, placing Ben
Grimm in the body of the Hulk, and
Dr Bruce Banner in the rock-hard
shell of the Thing. This set the Hulk
off on one of his trademark
rampages, storming through the city
and leaving rubble in his wake. The
Thing tried to subdue the Hulk, but
Mr Fantastic stepped in and
returned each man to his own body.
The Hulk was once again mild-
mannered Bruce Banner, and the
danger was averted – for a time.

Anger Management
The Hulk lives by his own rules, and is therefore constantly on the run from the authorities. On several occasions, the Thing has been called on to help bring the green goliath to justice.

Although each thinks he's the strongest, their fights always end in a stalemate.

Kindred Spirits

Both feared and hated by the general public due to their terrifying appearances, the Thing and the Hulk have more in common than they'd like to admit.

Wolverine

Although he considers himself a loner, Wolverine has been called on to team up with many other Super Heroes.

Born with the mutant ability to heal himself, lightning reflexes and razor sharp claws, Wolverine spent many years roaming the Canadian countryside and living off the land. However, when Charles Xavier recruited him to fight alongside his fellow mutants in the X-Men, Wolverine reluctantly accepted.

In time, he even became close friends with his teammates.

Throughout his long career, Wolverine has joined forces with many other Super Heroes. He fought corrupt soldiers with Spider-Man.

Super Strength
Wolverine's bones and claws were coated in an unbreakable metal known as adamantium in a government experiment.

He also helped Punisher to destroy a prison camp, and even battled a clan of evil ninjas known as the Hand with Captain America. Recently, he took up a place in the Avengers, alongside heroes such as Iron Man and Spider-Woman.

Daredevil
After he was brainwashed by the Hand, Wolverine found himself at odds with the Hand's most famous enemy, Daredevil.

Elektra
Wolverine and Elektra have paired together many times in the past, their merciless attitudes complementing each other perfectly.

Wolverine vs Hulk

Thanks to their short tempers, Wolverine and the incredible Hulk are often at each other's throats. It's brute strength versus speed and agility as these two try to prove which one is the most ferocious.

Tough Guy
Wolverine never backs down from a fight, even with a giant three times his size. In fact, those are the kind of odds that Wolverine lives for.

Scrapper
Wolverine's sharp claws can cut through anything, even the Hulk's thick, green hide.

When the Hulk accidentally collided with a passing airplane in the midst of one of his titanic jumps, Wolverine and his fellow X-Men managed to save the wrecked aircraft. However, in doing so one of the plane's engines crashed down to the earth and landed directly on the unsuspecting Hulk. Enraged by the pain, Hulk attacked Wolverine and goaded him into a fight. Clay Quartermain, Hulk's friend and travelling companion, interrupted the pair's vicious battle in the woods. Clay managed to calm the fiery pair down and Hulk and Wolverine parted ways. That wouldn't be the last time the short-tempered Super Heroes would meet as enemies.

Mood Swings
The Hulk has undergone many changes in personality. This is not good when he encounters Wolverine's hair-trigger temper.

Three's Company
Sent by the Canadian government to take down the Hulk, Wolverine interrupted the Hulk's fight with the wild Wendigo.

X-Men

Charles Xavier was born a mutant, with the power to read others' minds. In a world full of prejudice against mutants, Xavier decided to start a school to guide young mutants through life and to help teach them how to control their special talents. Xavier's recruits soon became known as the X-Men, a team of mutants sworn to protect a world that hates and fears them.

Magneto
Xavier's former friend, Magneto, has a different approach to mutant/human relations. He just wants to wipe out humanity.

The X-Men began as the small team of Cyclops, Marvel Girl, Beast, Iceman and Angel, and has grown to include dozens of other heroes, including Wolverine, Storm, Nightcrawler and Colossus.

Over the years, Xavier's simple dream of mutants and humans living together peacefully has shown signs of coming true. The X-Men have worked with many other Super Heroes and have even expanded into several other super teams, including X-Factor, the New Mutants and X-Force.

House Arrest
When dozens of mutants were locked in a government facility that was set to explode, the combined might of the X-Men and the Avengers saved them.

Sentinels
Constructed by the government, Sentinels were giant robots programmed to hunt down and destroy all mutants.

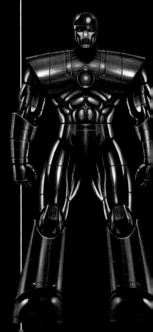

Dark Phoenix

When she was corrupted into the Dark Phoenix, Jean turned her costume to an ominous blood red shade.

The White Queen

Emma Frost, known as the White Queen, was a member of the Hellfire Club – the organisation responsible for tampering with Jean Grey's mind.

Dark Phoenix

When Marvel Girl, Jean Grey, was taken over by the entity known as the Phoenix Force, the X-Men faced perhaps their greatest challenge. Calling herself Phoenix, Jean fought alongside her fellow X-Men until her mind was tampered with by Jason Wyngarde, the villain known as Mastermind. Jean's enhanced powers soon became too much for her to handle, and she turned against her friends, wiping an entire world out of existence in the process.

Sacrifice
Jean threw herself in front of a giant laser cannon in order to do what she knew her teammates could not.

The X-Men then battled Phoenix, only to find themselves all captives of the Shi'ar Empire, an alien race determined to see Jean Grey destroyed. Under attack on the moon, Jean regained her true personality. Realising all the harm she'd done, Jean sacrificed herself in order to save her team and the universe from her terrible power.

Last Moments
Jean and Scott Summers, the mutant Cyclops, shared a heartfelt goodbye before Jean did what she had to.

Daredevil

As a child, Matt Murdock saved an elderly man's life by pushing him out of the path of a runaway truck. The truck crashed and spilt radioactive material near Matt's face. When he awoke later in hospital, Matt discovered that he was blind, but his other senses had been magnified tenfold. He could now hear a pin dropping a city block away, or read a newspaper simply by feeling the letters on the page. He also realised that he had a radar sense and could detect people and objects in his vicinity.

Neighbourhood Super Heroes
Spider-Man and Daredevil are both Manhattan residents so they often face the same villains, including Kingpin.

Later, Matt adopted a secret identity named Daredevil so that he could use his abilities to fight crime and protect his neighbourhood. In his civilian life, he is a lawyer. Although he has teamed up with many heroes as Daredevil, Matt has also represented some of them in court. As Daredevil he apprehends villains, and as Matt Murdock he sees that they're put away for good.

Punisher
Daredevil has tried to stop the Punisher several times over the years. He doesn't approve of the Punisher using deadly force.

Elektra
Elektra Natchios was Matt's first love. She became an assassin for hire after the death of her father.

The Kingpin

Turf War
At one point, Daredevil defeated the Kingpin. He claimed Hell's Kitchen for himself and cleaned up the neighbourhood.

No other villain has been more trouble for Daredevil than Wilson Fisk. Better known as the Kingpin, Fisk runs most of the organised crime in Manhattan, and has hundreds of criminals on his payroll.

When he heard rumours of the mysterious Elektra's superior fighting skills, the Kingpin hired her as his chief assassin. This angered a costumed criminal called Bullseye, who wanted the job for himself. Bullseye escaped from prison and attacked Elektra, killing her with one of her own weapons.

Elektra's murder hit her former love Daredevil hard. Raging Daredevil tracked down Bullseye, determined to make him pay for what he had done. It was the start of a long and bitter war between the two powerful individuals.

Although Elektra would later return from the grave, thanks to the Hand, her relationship with Daredevil could never be the same again.

Bullseye
Bullseye is blessed with perfect aim. He can turn anything, even a simple toothpick, into a lethal throwing dart.

Battleworld
Heroes from all walks of life found themselves suddenly appearing on Battleworld. As the war continued, new faces emerged, like that of Spider-Woman.

New Costume
When his old costume was destroyed in a fight, Spider-Man found a new one. He would later discover that his new costume was a living, breathing thing.

Secret Wars

The greatest heroes and villains in the universe found themselves engaged in the ultimate war when they were transported to a mysterious planet called Battleworld by an even more mysterious being called the Beyonder.

In order to observe the warriors in battle, the Beyonder promised to grant the winners anything their hearts desired. Dr Doom led his forces against those of Captain America and the two sides waged war. However, Dr Doom had bigger ideas and stole energy from the Beyonder so that he could take his place as the most powerful being in the universe. Thankfully, Captain America helped the Beyonder defeat Doom. Mr Fantastic then took advantage of all the residual energy and devised a way to return the heroes safely home.

The Beyonder
The Beyonder didn't show his face during the original Secret Wars, but, when he later travelled to Earth, he took on a human form.

Super Villains
Both old Spider-Man foes, the Lizard and Dr Octopus were just a few of the many villains in Dr Doom's army.

The Lizard   *Doctor Doom*   *Doctor Octopus*

The Surtur Saga

Thor, the Norse god of Thunder, had heard the legend of the powerful demon Surtur from his father Odin. Surtur was a powerful force for evil who wanted to conquer Earth. When Malekith the Accursed opened the magical Casket of Ancient Winters, releasing frigid cold temperatures throughout the earth, the time was right. With a sword mightier than even Thor's magic hammer, Surtur broke free from his own dimension and began to attack New York. Thor did his best to defend his adopted world from Surtur's forces, but he couldn't do it alone. Suddenly Odin appeared and managed to send the demon back to his own realm, but at a great cost – his life.

Forces of Thunder
Thor led an army composed of Super Heroes and gods to oppose this ancient evil.

Mjolnir
Thor used his magic hammer, Mjolnir, to knock Surtur's sword away and give his father the advantage he needed.

Thanos

Thanos literally fell in love with the being Death and was always trying to win her affections.

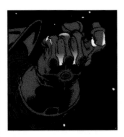

Infinity Gems

The gems granted their user control of the soul, the mind, power, time, reality and space.

Infinity Gauntlet

When the evil titan Thanos collected the fabled Infinity Gems, he became a near god-like being of great power. He placed the gems into a gauntlet he wore on his fist, and formed a palace that floated through space itself. Obsessed with death, Thanos began to destroy entire stars, which in turn wreaked havoc on the Earth.

Adam Warlock, heroes and villains united to storm Thanos's palace. Thanos disposed of them as if they were mere bugs. Later, tricked into leaving his body, Thanos lost his precious Infinity Gauntlet first to his former prisoner Nebula, and then to Adam Warlock. Warlock took the Gauntlet and set right all the things Thanos had destroyed. He returned all the Super Heroes but he now possessed the most powerful weapon in existence.

The Avengers
Although Captain America helped organise the attack, Thanos seemingly killed all the Avengers present.

Adam Warlock
Adam kept his plans to himself until the very end. He left the battle victorious, accompanied by his companions, Gamora and Pip the Troll.

The Avengers

They are the Earth's mightiest heroes. They serve as the first line of defence in a world overrun with Super Villains and monsters. They are the Avengers, and most Super Heroes consider it an honour even just to be near their ranks.

But when the Scarlet Witch, a longtime Avenger and trusted friend, could no longer cope with her vast reality-altering powers, the Super Hero team was literally ripped apart.

Scarlet Witch
With world-shaping abilities at her beck and call, the Scarlet Witch finally just lost control. It took nearly every single Avenger to bring her down.

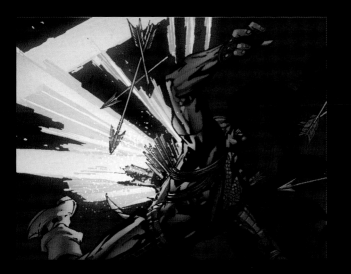

The Scarlet Witch went insane, and used her abilities to create false threats for the team, such as an army of evil robot Ultrons and a fleet of invading alien warships. With the help of sorcerer supreme Dr Strange, the Avengers discovered that the Scarlet Witch was behind the attacks. When confronted, the Scarlet Witch herself began to attack her fellow Avengers. The team managed to defeat their old ally, but then disbanded. This was one battle that simply hit too close to home for the Avengers.

The Roster
The original
Avengers were
Ant-Man, Thor,
the Hulk, the
Wasp and Iron
Man. Captain
America joined
the team early
on, and became
its leader.

House of M

After the Scarlet Witch's mental breakdown, the Avengers had handed her over to her father, Magneto, while they decided how she should be dealt with. But little did anyone know that the next morning they would wake up to find their lives completely different.

At the prompting of her brother and former hero, Quicksilver, the Scarlet Witch literally recreated the world into a reality that she preferred.

Royal Family
In the world the Scarlet Witch created, mutants ruled over humans. None were more powerful than Magneto's own royal family.

Layla Miller
A young girl named Layla Miller remembered the world as it was supposed to be. She used her abilities to unlock that knowledge in others.

It was a world designed to make all of her friends happy and content. In it, Spider-Man was married to his high school sweetheart, Wolverine was an agent of the government and Hawkeye was still alive.

The heroes eventually discovered that the world was not as it was supposed to be, and confronted the Scarlet Witch. When he learned what she had done, even Magneto turned on his daughter, forcing her to return the world to normal.

Quicksilver
Although he was behind the scheme to alter reality, Quicksilver's intentions were always to help his sister.

Angel

Ice Man

Black Widow

Hercules
Possessing strength to rival the mighty Thor, Hercules served as the team's resident muscle.

The Champions

A new Super Hero team was founded when former X-Men Iceman and Angel encountered a group of mythical harpies while walking on their college campus in California. The super spy Black Widow, demigod Hercules, and the demon-powered Ghost Rider all happened to be on the same campus and joined their fellow Super Heroes in the fight.

Ghost Rider

Hercules

The team realised there was a higher power behind the attack, and found themselves battling the god Pluto on top of Mount Olympus. Angel dubbed the victorious group the Champions.

The team only fought a few battles, but they managed to take on many high profile villains. They defeated Magneto, the Sentinels and Dr Doom before disbanding.

Born Leader
The Black Widow instinctively took on the leadership role for the Champions in the heat of their first battle.

Iron Man
Both a brilliant inventor and a millionaire, Tony Stark felt Super Heroes needed to change with the times.

Captain America
When the law agency S.H.I.E.L.D. asked Captain America to register with the government, Cap denied them, escaping on a nearby jet.

Road to Civil War

Captain America and Iron Man had been friends and close allies ever since the early days of the Avengers. But that was before the government passed the Superhuman Registration Act. The act made it illegal for costumed heroes to continue their wars on crime without first revealing their identities to the government.

With a firm belief in freedom of
choice, Captain America opposed
the act and became a fugitive from
the law. Iron Man saw the act as
the next logical step in fighting
crime, and revealed his identity.
The government then enlisted him
to arrest Captain America and all
who refused to comply with the act.

The battle lines were drawn.

Civil War

Revelation
In a press conference, Spider-Man revealed his identity to the entire world.

It was a war that pitted brother against brother and friend against friend. Captain America formed an underground resistance to oppose the government and the Superhuman Registration Act. Heroes like the Falcon, Daredevil and Cloak and Dagger joined his cause against Iron Man and his team of government supporters. Battles erupted all over the country, and many heroes fell.

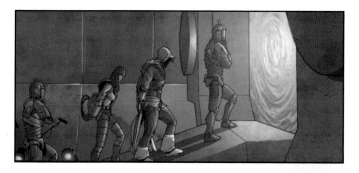

Negative Zone
Iron Man imprisoned heroes and villains alike in a dimension called the Negative Zone.

Some, like Spider-Man and the Invisible Woman, switched sides in the heat of battle to join Captain America's forces.

Eventually, Captain America surrendered, turning himself in to the government. And just like that, the war was over.

The world is a different place after the Civil War. Some heroes work for the government now, and

some remain in the shadows. But when there's danger, the differences fall away and all the forces for good unite. It is simply what they do, because they are the Super Heroes.

American Hero
Realising the fighting was doing more harm than good, Captain America turned himself in to Iron Man's forces.

Glossary

Aggression
A hostile, angry or destructive outlook on life.

Agility
The ability to move quickly, easily and gracefully.

Alter ego
A side of someone's personality that is different, such as a secret identity.

Cosmic
Relating to the whole universe, not just planet Earth.

Cosmos
The universe.

Endurance
The ability to withstand physical, and sometimes mental, pressures.

Entity
Something that exists – a living being or creature.

Ferocious
Extremely fierce and usually violent.

Force field
An invisible protective barrier that cannot be penetrated by weapons or bad guys.

Martial arts
Oriental forms of combat, such as karate. Martial arts can also be practised as sports.

Mutant
A human born with extraordinary features or special powers.

Radar
An electronic system that detects the presence of ships, aircraft etc, using radio waves.

Radiation
Energy emitted in the form of waves or particles.

Radioactive
A way of describing an element that spontaneously emits rays that are often harmful.

Solar energy
Power that comes from the sun.

Stealth
The ability to move quietly and cautiously to avoid being detected.

Super Hero
A man, woman or alien with special powers and abilities. A Super Hero uses his or her powers for good – to protect innocent people and worlds and to fight evil.

Super Hero team
A group of Super Heroes who work together e.g. the Avengers, the X-Men and the Fantastic Four. Super Heroes become even stronger when they work together.

Super Villain
Also a man, woman or alien with special powers and abilities. However, a Super Villain uses his or her abilities for evil – to gain power and harm innocent people.

Symbiote
Two different creatures bond together to form a new entity.

Telekinesis
The ability to move objects just with the powers of the mind.

Telepathy
The ability to read the thoughts and feelings of other people.

Teleport
To travel a great distance in an instant. This could be done with a machine or simply by disappearing from one place and then reappearing in another, a moment later. Unfortunately, only some Super Heroes can do this.